NOW YOU CAN READ ABOUT....
BIG CATS

TEXT BY RITA GRAINGE

ILLUSTRATED BY GRAHAM ALLEN

BRIMAX BOOKS • NEWMARKET • ENGLAND

Do you have a pet cat?
Family cats have soft fur coats.
They eat fish and canned food.
They purr and hiss and meow.
Their claws stay sharp because
they pull them into their paws.

They love
to curl up
in a chair
by the fire.

Big cats also have soft fur coats. They hide their claws. They purr when they are happy. But big cats do not eat food from a can. They feed by killing and eating other animals. They do not curl up in chairs. Big cats live in the wild. They are not tame like a pet cat. Look at this lion roaring.

There are 30 kinds
of wild cats.
The tiger is the
biggest of the
wild cats. It is
very strong. Look
at this tiger
standing on its
back legs.

Cheetahs can run faster than any
other animal. They can run as
fast as 60 miles per hour.

Look how high
this puma is
jumping.

A bobcat looks
like a big pet
cat. But it is
strong. It can
kill a goat.

The lynx looks
like the bobcat.
It has a longer
tail. The lynx has
very good eyesight.

Baby wild cats are called cubs. They are born blind. These two leopard cubs are asleep. The female leopard is looking after them. She is trying to scare away the wild dogs.

Look at these
jaguar cubs. They
have spotted coats
like the leopards.
Can you see the
jaguar cub trying
to climb the rock?
One cub is playing
with a turtle.

These ocelot cubs
are safe in their
den. It is in
a hollow tree.

Many big cats hunt alone. Tigers sleep during the day and hunt at night. Tigers roam for miles. They also love to swim. In hot places like India, tigers cool off in the river.

Some big cats hunt in trees. This jaguar is chasing monkeys.

Look at the jaguar hanging over the water. It kills fish with its paws.

Leopards leap down on animals.

Most of the big cats live alone.

Snow leopards live
in cold snowy
lands. Their thick
fur keeps them
warm.

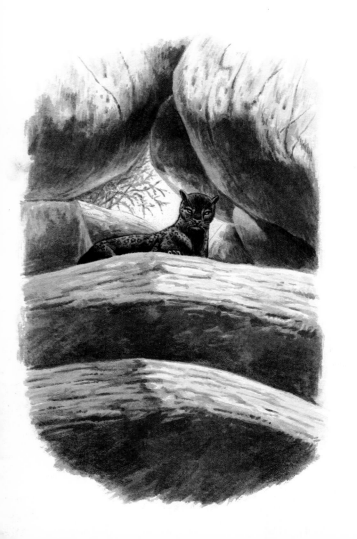

Black leopards
are called
panthers. Can you
see the panther
hiding among the
rocks?

These big cats live in America.

Some jaguars live on mountains. Others live in forests. They like to be near water.

The puma is also called the cougar. Another name for it is mountain lion. Which name do you like best?

Lions live and hunt together.
A pack of lions is called a pride.
As many as 30 lions are in one
pride. Look at this lion family.
They are resting in the shade of
a tree. The cubs are drinking.
The male lion keeps the family
safe from attack.

The lioness is hunting for food. Can you see her hunting the zebras? She keeps low down. She is driving the zebras towards the rest of the pride. They are hidden in the grass.

All big cats have coats which help them to hide. Look at this dark jungle. Can you see the tiger? Its striped coat is not easy to see in the jungle.

The striped coat also helps the tiger to hide in the long grass.

Snow leopards have
pale spotted fur.
It helps them to
hide among rocks.

Black panthers
hunt at night
when it is very
dark. Look closely.

This leopard is
hiding among the
leaves and twigs.

Now there are fewer wild cats. When the trees are chopped down or burnt by fires the big cats have nowhere to live. For many years people have hunted big cats.

Some people hunt big cats for sport. Other people kill big cats for their skins. The skins are made into rugs or fur coats. Look for the tiger in the net.

Many big cats are killed. Very soon there may be no more big cats left. We must look after all the big cats. You can visit these lovely animals in zoos or on game reserves. The World Wildlife Fund helps to look after them.

In India people are not allowed
to kill tigers and leopards.
These big cats live in large
areas of wild country. No one can
visit them. The big cats can live
free from danger.

In this book you have read about big cats. Do you know what these are called?